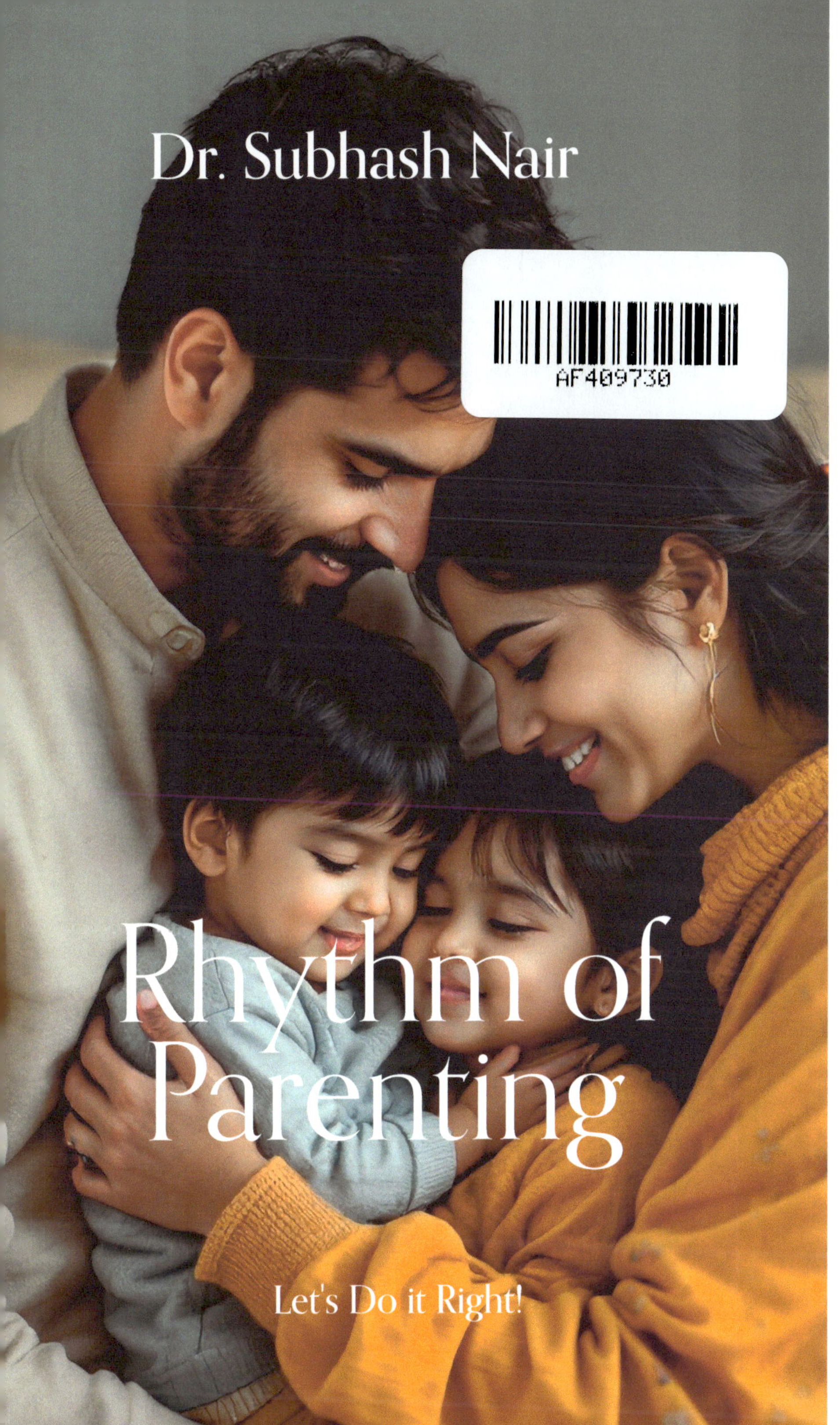
Dr. Subhash Nair
AF409730
Rhythm of
Parenting
Let's Do it Right!

Produced, edited, and designed by Dr. Subhash Nair
First edition in 2025

In today's fast-paced world, the struggle to maintain a balanced emotional state among teenagers is a genuine concern for Indian parents, who often feel overwhelmed by disturbing media narratives. The rhythm of parenting in such times demands a discerning eye and a nurturing touch. With the cacophony of media-driven fears, parents must orchestrate a harmonious environment that not only shields but also empowers their children. Understanding and adapting to the subtle rhythms of evolving family dynamics becomes crucial in fostering resilience against external turmoil. This book delves into the intricacies of emotional well-being, offering a practical guide to navigating the tumultuous landscape of adolescence. By embracing culturally resonant strategies and time-tested wisdom, Indian parents can learn to discern the signals within the noise, leading their teenagers with assurance and empathy. By harmonizing traditional values with contemporary challenges, this book provides parents with tools to cultivate emotional intelligence and fortitude in their children. As we explore the rhythm of parenting, the ensuing chapters will equip you with actionable insights and strategies to foster open communication and understanding. This authoritative guide is designed to empower parents, transforming anxieties into opportunities for growth and connection, ultimately fostering a secure and nurturing environment for your teenager's development.

Dr. Subhash Nair

Rhythm of Parenting

Let's Do it Right!

Dedicated to

- Smt. Vijaya B. Nair, my loving mother and first teacher.
- Late Shri. T.G. Bhaskaran Nair, my father and source of inspiration.
- Delightful teacher colleagues with whom I associated, worked, and collaborated.
- Smt. Jayasree Subhash, my partner in life and a delightful teacher, who supported all my experiments and guided me with valuable inputs and feedback.
- Our children, Mr. Shyam S. Nair, an ardent educationist, and Mrs. Varsha Venugopal, who always encouraged me to be myself in work and life.
- Our children, Mrs. Sreesha S. Nair, and Mr. Anil S. Nair, Engineers, who always encouraged me to be fair and objective.
- Our grandsons, Parth Nair and Aarav Nair, who are our source of unlimited love, affection, and creativity.
- Members of our families who appreciated and supported my life, work, and efforts.

Summary

I

Emotional Building Blocks

1.1 - Parenting in India

Parenting in India requires a deep understanding of emotional development within children, especially when considering the broader social issues that affect family life. These include the pervasive presence of social violence that families must navigate. This chapter delves into the intricate dance of nurturing emotional intelligence and resilience in children against the backdrop of external challenges. It explores how these emotional building blocks are not just essential for individual growth but also play a crucial role in coping with societal pressures. The following discussion will explore strategies Indian parents can employ to foster emotional strength in their children while addressing the impact of social violence. By examining the dynamics of empathy, emotional regulation, and resilience within the home environment, this chapter seeks to provide readers with actionable insights and guidance. We will also investigate the influence of cultural norms on parenting practices and present ways to safeguard children from the adverse effects of violence. The role of community support and systemic changes in supporting safer family experiences will be examined, along with educational approaches to promote peace and empathy among younger generations.

1.2 - Emotional Building Blocks in Parenting

Nurturing emotional intelligence in children is an essential component of effective parenting, especially in today's world where socio-emotional skills play a pivotal role in navigating life's challenges. Understanding and cultivating emotional intelligence involves recognizing, understanding, and managing one's emotions and those of others, forming the foundation for healthy interpersonal relationships (Salovey & Mayer, 1990). Research underscores that children with high emotional intelligence are better equipped to communicate effectively, maintain positive relationships, and manage stress and adversity ("Nurturing Emotional Intelligence in Children: A Guide for Parents and Guardians," 2025).

The cultivation of empathy stands as a cornerstone in emotional intelligence development. Teaching children to identify with others' feelings fosters compassion and enhances their ability to engage in meaningful, emotionally intelligent interactions from an early age. Empathy allows children to step into the shoes of others, promoting understanding and reducing instances of conflict. Parents can encourage this by modeling empathetic behavior themselves and engaging children in perspective-taking activities (Eisenberg et al., 2006). For instance, discussing how characters in stories might feel and encouraging children to express how they would respond to various situations helps solidify these concepts.

Parenting strategies aimed at promoting emotional self-regulation are critical for helping children maintain emotional balance and effectively cope with stress. Techniques like deep breathing,

Creating a home environment that supports emotional resilience is another crucial aspect of nurturing emotional intelligence. Emotional resilience involves the ability to recover from setbacks and maintain mental health despite adversities. Parents play a significant role in developing this trait by creating a supportive atmosphere that encourages open communication and validates children's feelings (Denham et al.,

counting to ten, or taking breaks when overwhelmed are practical ways parents can teach emotional regulation (Raver et al., 2011). These strategies are not only about avoiding negative emotions but also about understanding and working through them constructively. By doing so, children learn to navigate challenges without being consumed by anxiety or frustration.

2012). Sharing personal experiences about overcoming difficulties can inspire children and show them that it's possible to grow stronger from life's challenges.

Furthermore, mindful parenting practices offer a holistic approach to fostering emotional intelligence. Mindful parenting emphasizes presence, awareness, and empathy in parent-child interactions, enhancing both the emotional well-being of children and parents. Research indicates that parents practicing mindfulness are more emotionally regulated, thereby modeling these behaviors for their children (Center, 2023). This practice includes active listening, where parents fully focus on their child's words and feelings, validating their experiences and fostering emotional security.

Encouraging emotional expression is equally important. Creating a safe space where children feel comfortable discussing their feelings, thoughts, and concerns promotes openness and honesty. Positive reinforcement can further support this by acknowledging and celebrating children's achievements and efforts, boosting their self-esteem and reinforcing positive emotional patterns.

Self-compassion is another vital element children learn from observing their parents. Parents who model kindness towards themselves in challenging times provide a powerful example for their children. This modeling shows children it's okay to acknowledge emotions and treat oneself gently rather than harshly.

1.3 - Impact of Social Violence on Parenting in India

In India, social violence persists as a complex fabric interwoven into daily life and family dynamics. Understanding how this pervasive issue influences parenting practices and child development is crucial, especially given its various manifestations, such as domestic abuse, community conflicts, and systemic discrimination.

Prevalence of Social Violence: Domestic abuse remains a significant issue in many Indian homes, where traditional power structures often dictate the roles and behaviors of family members. This form of violence disrupts the emotional and physical safety within families, leading to an environment fraught with tension and fear. In communities, conflicts over resources, caste-based discrimination, and religious tensions can spill into neighborhoods, affecting children who witness or are caught in the crossfire. Systemic issues like economic disparities further exacerbate these situations, with marginalized communities bearing the brunt of violence. According to Fernandes et al. (2021), socioeconomic hardship in urban slums elevates risks for child maltreatment, affecting family dynamics and child development.

Impact on Children: Exposure to violence can have profound effects on children's psychological health. When children grow up witnessing violence, they may develop heightened anxiety and fear, which can manifest in numerous ways, from behavioral issues to problems with concentration and learning. This constant state of alertness impacts their ability to trust others and form healthy relationships, potentially affecting their long-term well-being. Studies highlight that adverse childhood experiences, including exposure to violence, can lead to increased risk factors for mortality in adulthood (Fernandes et al., 2021).

Cultural Norms and Societal Expectations: Cultural attitudes towards discipline in India sometimes perpetuate cycles of violence. Traditional disciplinary methods, often physical, are ingrained in societal norms and passed down generations. These practices are reinforced by societal expectations that uphold strict disciplinary measures as necessary for cultivating respect and obedience in children. However, these approaches can hinder children's emotional growth, teaching them to associate love with fear and compliance rather than understanding and mutual respect. When cultural norms endorse harsh disciplinary practices, parents might struggle to adopt more nurturing and supportive parenting styles.

Strategies for Protection: To shield children from the adverse effects of social violence, parents can implement several protective strategies. Creating safe and supportive home environments is paramount. Parents should foster open communication, allowing children to express their fears and anxieties without judgment. By encouraging dialogue, parents help children process their emotions and foster resilience. Additionally, seeking support from community resources, such as counseling services and support groups, can provide families with essential tools to manage stress and conflict effectively. These resources offer guidance on non-violent communication and conflict resolution, promoting healthier family dynamics.

Engagement with community initiatives aimed at reducing violence is also critical. Programs that focus on educating parents about the impacts of violence on child development can shift attitudes towards more peaceful parenting approaches. Furthermore, strengthening family bonds through shared activities and positive reinforcement can help counteract the negative effects of external violence. By prioritizing emotional connections and understanding, parents cultivate a sense of security and stability for their children.

Addressing systemic issues is just as important in mitigating the influence of social violence. Promoting awareness of children's rights and advocating for policy changes that protect children from violence, such as stricter enforcement of laws against domestic abuse and child protection legislation, can create safer environments for children. Organizations like UNICEF emphasize the importance of implementing policies that safeguard children's rights, ensuring they grow up in nurturing family environments (UNICEF, n.d.).

Moreover, education plays a pivotal role in preventing violence. Schools can serve as safe havens, teaching children about empathy, respect, and conflict resolution. By incorporating these lessons into curricula, educational institutions contribute to shaping a generation that values peace and equality. Empowering children with knowledge and skills to cope with adversity prepares them to break cycles of violence and build supportive communities.

1.4 Final Insights

In this chapter, we examined the pivotal role emotional intelligence plays in parenting and its influence within the Indian landscape, where social violence can significantly impact child development. Emotional intelligence fosters empathy, self-regulation, and resilience, equipping children with vital life skills to navigate complex social environments. By nurturing these traits, parents not only promote healthier interpersonal relationships but also empower their children to tackle challenges without being overwhelmed by fear or anxiety. The strategies discussed, such as mindful parenting and fostering open communication, serve as essential tools for parents aiming to provide a supportive home environment that counteracts the negative effects of societal pressures and traditional disciplinary norms.

Addressing the profound impact of social violence on family dynamics in India calls for urgent attention. Parents must adopt protective strategies to shield their children from the adverse effects of witnessing violence, promoting open dialogue and seeking community support. Encouraging non-violent communication and participating in initiatives that educate and shift parenting attitudes towards more compassionate approaches are crucial steps. Furthermore, advocating for policy changes and leveraging educational systems to impart values of empathy and respect can lay the groundwork for a future generation that champions peace and equality. Through these concerted efforts, families can break cycles of violence and cultivate environments where children thrive emotionally and mentally.

1.5 Reference

Center. (2023). "Mindful Parenting: Nurturing Emotional Intelligence in Children." Center for Spiritual Living Minneapolis. https://www.cslminneapolis.org/news/mindful-parenting-nurturing-emotional-intelligence-in-children

Fernandes, G., Fernandes, M., Vaidya, N., De Souza, P., Plotnikova, E., Geddes, R., Holla, B., Sharma, E., Benegal, V., & Choudhry, V. (2021, August 8).

Through classroom teachings and community programs, children can learn the importance of understanding and kindness, equipping them to become catalysts for peace and equality.

Prevalence of child maltreatment in India and its association with gender, urbanisation and policy: a rapid review and meta-analysis protocol. BMJ Open. https://doi.org/10.1136/bmjopen-2020-044983

Nurturing Emotional Intelligence in Children: A Guide for Parents and Guardians. (2025). Littlebeamfoundation.com. https://www.littlebeamfoundation.com/news/nurturing-emotional-intelligence-in-children-a-guide-for-parents-and-guardians

UNICEF. (n.d.). Child protection. Www.unicef.org. https://www.unicef.org/india/what-we-do/child-protection

2

Emotional Development

Emotional development is a complex and continuous process that unfolds throughout childhood and adolescence. It's not a linear staircase but rather a dynamic journey with periods of rapid growth, plateaus, and even temporary regressions. Understanding these stages is crucial for parents, educators, and anyone working with young people. Here's a description of emotional development stages from early childhood to late adolescence, highlighting key milestones and characteristics:

2.1 -Early Childhood (Infancy – 5 Years)

Infancy (0-18 months): Foundational Emotions and Attachment

Basic Emotions: Infants are born with the capacity to express basic emotions like joy, sadness, anger, fear, surprise, and disgust. These are largely instinctual and communicated nonverbally (facial expressions, cries, body language).

Emotional Contagion: Infants are highly sensitive to the emotions of their caregivers, mirroring and reacting to them.

Early Self-Awareness: Around 18 months, infants begin to develop a sense of self, recognising themselves as separate from others. This is evident in mirror recognition and the use of "me" and "mine."

Attachment Formation: The primary emotional task of infancy is forming a secure attachment with primary caregivers Consistent, responsive, and nurturing care fosters secure attachment, providing a foundation of trust and security that impacts later emotional development. Insecure attachment can develop from inconsistent or neglectful caregiving, leading to anxiety or avoidance in relationships.

Toddlerhood (18 months – 3 years): Emergence of Self-Conscious Emotions and Autonomy

Self-Conscious Emotions: As toddlers develop a stronger sense of self, self-conscious emotions emerge, such as shame, embarrassment, pride, and guilt. These emotions require self-reflection and an understanding of social standards. They are often tied to caregiver approval or disapproval.

Developing Emotional Vocabulary: Toddlers begin to use language to label their own emotions and the emotions of others. Emotional literacy starts to build through caregiver modelling and direct teaching.

Emotional Regulation Begins (Rudimentary): Toddlers start to develop rudimentary emotional regulation skills, though they are still heavily reliant on caregivers for co-regulation. Tantrums and emotional outbursts are common as they learn to manage strong feelings.

Autonomy vs. Shame and Doubt (Erikson's Stage): This stage is marked by the drive for autonomy and independence. Successful navigation leads to feelings of self-reliance; failure can lead to feelings of shame and doubt about their abilities.

Preschool Years (3-5 years): Emotional Understanding and Socialization

Increased Emotional Understanding:

Preschoolers develop a better understanding of their own and others' emotions. They can start to recognise different emotions in facial expressions and situations.

Emotional Complexity: They begin to grasp that people can experience multiple emotions at once or have mixed feelings.

Developing Empathy and Perspective-Taking: Empathy starts to emerge as preschoolers become more aware of others' feelings and can begin to take their perspective (though still egocentric to some extent).

Emotional Regulation Improvement: Emotional regulation skills improve, although preschoolers still struggle with impulse control and managing intense emotions. They learn strategies like distraction, self-soothing (thumb-sucking, comfort objects), and seeking caregiver comfort.

Socialisation of Emotions: Preschoolers learn about social rules regarding emotional expression. They begin to understand which emotions are acceptable to express in different contexts and how to express them in socially appropriate ways (influenced by culture, family, and peer interactions).

Initiative vs. Guilt (Erikson's Stage): Preschoolers take initiative in play and activities. Success fosters a sense of purpose and initiative; failure or discouragement can lead to feelings of guilt and inhibition.

2.2 -Middle Childhood (6-12 Years)

Emotional Complexity and Nuance: Children in middle childhood understand more complex emotions like jealousy, anxiety, and frustration in nuanced ways. They can differentiate between pride and arrogance, shame and guilt.

Improved Emotional Regulation: Emotional regulation skills become significantly more sophisticated. Children develop strategies like cognitive reappraisal (changing how they think about a situation), problem-solving, and seeking social support to manage emotions.

Understanding Mixed Emotions: Children grasp that people can experience conflicting emotions simultaneously (e.g., feeling happy and sad at the same time).

Increased Empathy and Perspective-Taking: Empathy deepens, and children become better at understanding others' perspectives and feelings, even when different from their own. This contributes to improved social skills and peer relationships.

Self-Conscious Emotions and Social Comparison: Self-conscious emotions become more internally driven (less reliant on external approval). Children engage in social comparison, evaluating themselves and their emotions relative to peers, which can impact self-esteem and social anxiety.

Industry vs. Inferiority (Erikson's Stage): Middle childhood is focused on developing a sense of competence and industry through school, hobbies, and activities. Success leads to feelings of mastery and competence; failure or repeated setbacks can lead to feelings of inferiority and inadequacy.

2.3-Adolescence (13-18+ Years)

Early Adolescence (12-14 years): Emotional Intensity and Fluctuations

Emotional Volatility and Intensity: Early adolescence is often characterised by heightened emotional intensity and rapid shifts in mood. Hormonal changes, identity exploration, and social pressures contribute to this emotional rollercoaster.

Increased Self-Consciousness and Body Image Concerns: Adolescents become acutely aware of themselves and how they are perceived by others. Body image issues, social anxiety, and concerns about peer acceptance are common.

Identity Exploration Begins: Adolescents begin to grapple with questions of "Who am I?" and explore different aspects of their identity, which can be emotionally charged and sometimes confusing.

Peer Influence and Conformity: Peer relationships become paramount, and there is strong pressure to conform to peer norms and expectations, including emotional expression.

Struggle with Emotional Regulation: While emotional regulation skills are more developed than in childhood, early adolescence can be a time of emotional dysregulation due to the intensity of emotions and the challenges of navigating new social and identity demands.

Middle Adolescence (15-17 years): Identity Development and Deeper Relationships

Identity Exploration Deepens: Adolescents actively explore different roles, values, beliefs, and ideologies to solidify their sense of self. This can involve experimentation and some emotional turmoil.

Increased Abstract Thought About Emotions: Adolescents develop the capacity for more abstract thought about emotions, reflecting on their feelings, understanding their origins, and considering the perspectives of others in more complex emotional situations.

Deeper Romantic Relationships: Romantic relationships often become more significant, bringing new emotional experiences and challenges related to intimacy, commitment, and rejection.

Emotional Regulation Continues to Develop: Emotional regulation skills become more refined, though adolescents may still struggle with impulse control and managing intense emotions in certain situations (e.g., conflicts, romantic disappointments).

Intimacy vs. Isolation (Erikson's Stage – Late Adolescence/Early Adulthood): While technically bridging into late adolescence, the focus on developing intimate relationships begins in middle adolescence. Adolescents seek deeper connections and fear isolation if unable to form meaningful bonds.

Late Adolescence (18+ years): Emotional Maturity and Autonomy

Emotional Maturity and Stability: Emotional experiences become more stable and less volatile as emotional regulation skills are further refined, and identity becomes more solidified.

Autonomous Emotional Functioning: Late adolescents become more emotionally independent from parents and family, relying more on their own internal resources and coping mechanisms.

Established Identity: A more coherent and stable sense of identity is generally achieved, although identity development is a lifelong process.

Future-Orientated Thinking and Emotional Planning: Adolescents begin to think more about their future goals, aspirations, and life paths, and their emotions become increasingly linked to these considerations (e.g., anxiety about college applications, excitement about career prospects).

Intimate Relationships and

Commitment: Late adolescence and early adulthood are marked by the development of intimate relationships characterised by deeper emotional sharing, commitment, and interdependence.

Generativity vs. Stagnation (Erikson's Stage – Early Adulthood): While this stage is primarily in early adulthood, late adolescence lays the groundwork for thinking about contributing to society and future generations.

2.4-Important Considerations:

Individual Variation: Emotional development is highly individual. Children and adolescents progress at different paces, and there is a wide range of what is considered "typical."

Cultural Influences: Culture significantly shapes emotional expression, understanding, and regulation. What is considered acceptable or normative emotional behaviour varies across cultures.

Context and Situation: Emotional responses are always influenced by context and situation. A child's emotional behaviour will differ depending on who they are with, where they are, and what is happening.

Interconnectedness: Emotional development is deeply intertwined with cognitive, social, and physical development. Progress in one area influences and is influenced by progress in others.

Ongoing Process: Emotional development continues throughout adulthood. While the most dramatic changes occur during childhood and adolescence, we continue to learn, adapt, and refine our emotional skills throughout life.

Understanding these stages provides a framework for appreciating the remarkable journey of emotional growth from infancy to adulthood. It allows parents, educators, and caregivers to provide appropriate support, guidance, and understanding at each stage, fostering healthy emotional development and wellbeing.

Understanding the developmental stages allows parents to build strong emotional foundations for their children, enhancing their capability to form meaningful relationships and cope with life's challenges.

The Foundation of Emotional Well-being

- Emotional Awareness and Identification
- Emotional Regulation
- Empathy
- Perspective-Taking
- Resilience

Parenting Rhythm and Emotional Skill Development Examples

- Predictable routines (meal times, bedtime)
- Consistent responses to emotions (comforting a crying child)
- Regular quality time and connection

Disruptions in Rhythm and Emotional Challenges
Impact of Chaotic/ Erratic Rhythms

• Increased Anxiety and Fear
• Difficulty in Regulating Emotions
• Attachment Issues
• Increased Behavioral Problems
• Resilience

Understanding Generational Differences

3.1 - Generational Differences

Understanding generational differences is integral to grasping the ever-evolving fabric of our society. Each generation comes with its own set of experiences, values, and worldviews, shaped profoundly by the historical events, cultural shifts, and technological advancements they encounter. By examining these factors, we can discern why individuals from different age groups might perceive the world uniquely. This insight not only fosters empathy but also aids in bridging the gap between generations, allowing for more effective communication and cooperation. Recognizing these variances helps us appreciate the diverse ways in which people contribute to social and cultural development, enriching our collective existence.

In this chapter, we embark on an exploration of diverse generations such as the Lost Generation, Greatest Generation, Silent Generation, and Baby Boomers, while further delving into modern cohorts like Generation X, Millennials, Generation Z, and Generation Alpha. Each section will unveil the distinctive characteristics, societal roles, and influences of these groups, offering a comprehensive understanding of how they have interacted with the world around them. We shall examine their unique responses to economic conditions, technological changes, and cultural dynamics. This journey through time promises to enhance our comprehension of intergenerational relationships and the distinct imprint each generation leaves upon the world.

3.2 - Generations Over Time: A Historical Perspective

Understanding Generational Differences

To understand the unique characteristics and societal influences of earlier generations, it's crucial to first consider their historical contexts. Each generation is shaped by the significant events, cultural shifts, and technological advancements of its time. In this section, we explore the defining traits of the Lost Generation, the Greatest Generation, the Silent Generation, and the Baby Boomers, providing a foundation for understanding their collective impact on society.

The Lost Generation, born approximately between 1883 and 1900, came of age during World War I and the Roaring Twenties. This group is marked by a sense of disillusionment and existential reflection following the devastation of war. Originally termed by Gertrude Stein and popularized through Ernest Hemingway's literature, they found themselves questioning traditional values and experimenting culturally in response to a world that seemed chaotic and unpredictable. Notable figures like F. Scott Fitzgerald and Gertrude Stein exemplify the era's artistic rebellion and pursuit of new meaning in life. The tumultuous times fostered a spirit of innovation and artistic expression, which became hallmarks of their cultural influence (Know Your Generations, n.d.).

overcoming adversity. This generation's perseverance laid the groundwork for social and economic recovery, leading to prosperity in the subsequent decades. Influential members such as Nelson Mandela and Queen Elizabeth II exemplify their strong principles and dedication to community welfare (The Classification and

Following the Lost Generation, the Greatest Generation, born from 1901 to 1927, faced the Great Depression and the trials of World War II. Known for their resilience and determination, they contributed significantly to the war effort and post-war reconstruction. Their experiences during these challenging periods instilled a profound sense of duty, self-sacrifice, and a collective approach to

Characteristics of Different Generations: A Journey over the Years, 2024).

In contrast, the Silent Generation, born between 1928 and 1945, grew up in an era characterized by both post-war affluence and stringent social conformity. Despite having witnessed significant global conflict in their early years, this generation often found themselves in quieter roles compared to their predecessors. Many members of this generation adopted conservative values and adhered to societal norms to maintain stability and security during uncertain times. They experienced the prosperity of the 1950s but also navigated the cultural tensions of the McCarthy era. Icons such as Martin Luther King Jr. and Ruth Bader Ginsburg stand out as figures who later advocated for change, despite the overall atmosphere of restraint during their formative years (Know Your Generations, n.d.).

Lastly, the Baby Boomer generation, born approximately between 1946 and 1964, emerged during an iconic period of change and optimism. Following World War II, there was a significant increase in birth rates, contributing to this generation's name. Baby Boomers experienced incredible economic growth, widespread suburban development, and powerful social movements for civil rights. This era is defined by its transformative approaches to traditional norms, including progressive efforts toward gender equality, racial justice, and environmental awareness. As products of a booming economy, they had access to better education and job opportunities, fueling their ambitions and broadening societal expectations. Figures like Barack Obama and Hillary Clinton personify their drive for social progression and leadership (The Classification and Characteristics of Different Generations: A Journey over the Years, 2024).

3.3 - Modern Generations: Technological Influences and Cultural Evolution

In today's rapidly changing world, understanding how different generations adapt to technological advancements and cultural trends is crucial. Each generation possesses unique characteristics shaped by the societal contexts in which they grew up. This exploration focuses on Generation X, Millennials (Generation Y), Generation Z, and Generation Alpha, addressing their distinct traits and how they interact with technology and culture.

Generation X, born approximately between 1965 and 1980, emerged during a period of economic transition and social change. Often described as independent and skeptical, this generation was shaped by higher divorce rates and frequent economic shifts. As children, Gen Xers experienced a rise in dual-income households, leading to an emphasis on self-reliance. Consequently, they developed a pragmatic approach to life, valuing work-life balance long before it became a popular concept. This generation witnessed the birth of personal computing and the internet, positioning them as the bridge between the analog past and the digital future.

Next, Millennials, or Generation Y, born between 1981 and 1996, are digital natives who have been instrumental in driving the technological revolution. Growing up alongside the rapid development of the internet, smartphones, and social media, Millennials seamlessly integrate technology into their daily lives. This generation values diversity and inclusion and often advocates for social justice causes. They demand workplaces that offer flexibility and purpose, while also seeking meaningful connections both online and offline. As such, Millennials have revolutionized industries through their affinity for technology and entrepreneurship, shaping modern workplace dynamics.

Following Millennials, Generation Z encompasses individuals born approximately between 1997 and 2012. Having never known a world without the internet, this generation has grown up deeply embedded in a technologically saturated environment. Instant communication via messaging apps and social media platforms is second nature to them. Their awareness of global issues, coupled with a strong desire for authenticity, makes them outspoken advocates for change. This generation's commitment to social justice is apparent in their willingness to challenge existing norms and demand accountability from corporations and governments alike (Khan, 2024).

Lastly, Generation Alpha, born from 2013 onwards, represents the first cohort entirely born in the 21st century. Growing up in a fully digital world, Gen Alpha is expected to be the most technologically immersed generation thus far. With early exposure to AI devices and smart technologies, these children are developing an intuitive understanding of digital environments. Although still in their formative years, projections suggest that they will approach education and employment with unprecedented adaptability and creativity. The emphasis on critical thinking, creativity, and emotional intelligence will be paramount as they navigate a future defined by technological advancements and automation (Casey, 2024).

3.4 - Bringing It All Together

In exploring the diverse characteristics and societal impacts of generations from the Lost Generation to Generation Z, this chapter underscores how each group has been molded by their unique historical and cultural contexts. The earlier generations experienced significant world events that shaped their values and contributions to society, while modern generations navigate an ever-evolving digital landscape that influences their outlooks and behaviors. Understanding these generational differences is essential for recognizing how past experiences and present technological advancements intersect, ultimately shaping our collective future.

For Indian parents, insights into these generational traits provide valuable context for appreciating how each cohort's experiences influence their perspectives on family, career, and community engagement. As India continues to evolve technologically and culturally, being aware of generational nuances can foster better communication and understanding across age groups. By bridging generational divides through awareness, parents can guide their children in navigating contemporary challenges while respecting the rich tapestry of Indian tradition intertwined with global influences.

3.5 -Reference

Casey, A. E. (2024, October 22). The Impact of Social Media and Technology on Gen Alpha. The Annie E. Casey Foundation. https://www.aecf.org/blog/impact-of-social-media-on-gen-alpha

Khan, M. (2024, May 26). Gen Z and Gen Alpha. Medium. https://medium.com/@Mahi_khan/gen-z-and-gen-alpha-135e287c36c1

Know Your Generations. (n.d.). San Francisco Supervisor Joel Engardio. https://engardio.com/blog/generations

The classification and characteristics of different generations: a journey over the years. (2024, May 13). Www.enelgreenpower.com. https://www.enelgreenpower.com/learning-hub/gigawhat/search-articles/articles/2024/05/classification-generations-x-y-z-alpha

Modern generations face the unprecedented wave of a digital era, reshaping human interaction and worldview in ways unimaginable to their predecessors.

TRANSFORM-ED

Generation Nomenclature

Missionary Generation (1860-1882)

Lost Generation (1883-1900)

Greatest Generation (1901-1927)

Silent Generation (1928-1945)

Boomers (1946-1964)

Gen X (1965-1980)

Gen Y, Millennials (1981-1996)

Gen Z, Zoomers, iGen (1997-2012)

Gen Alpha (2013-2025)

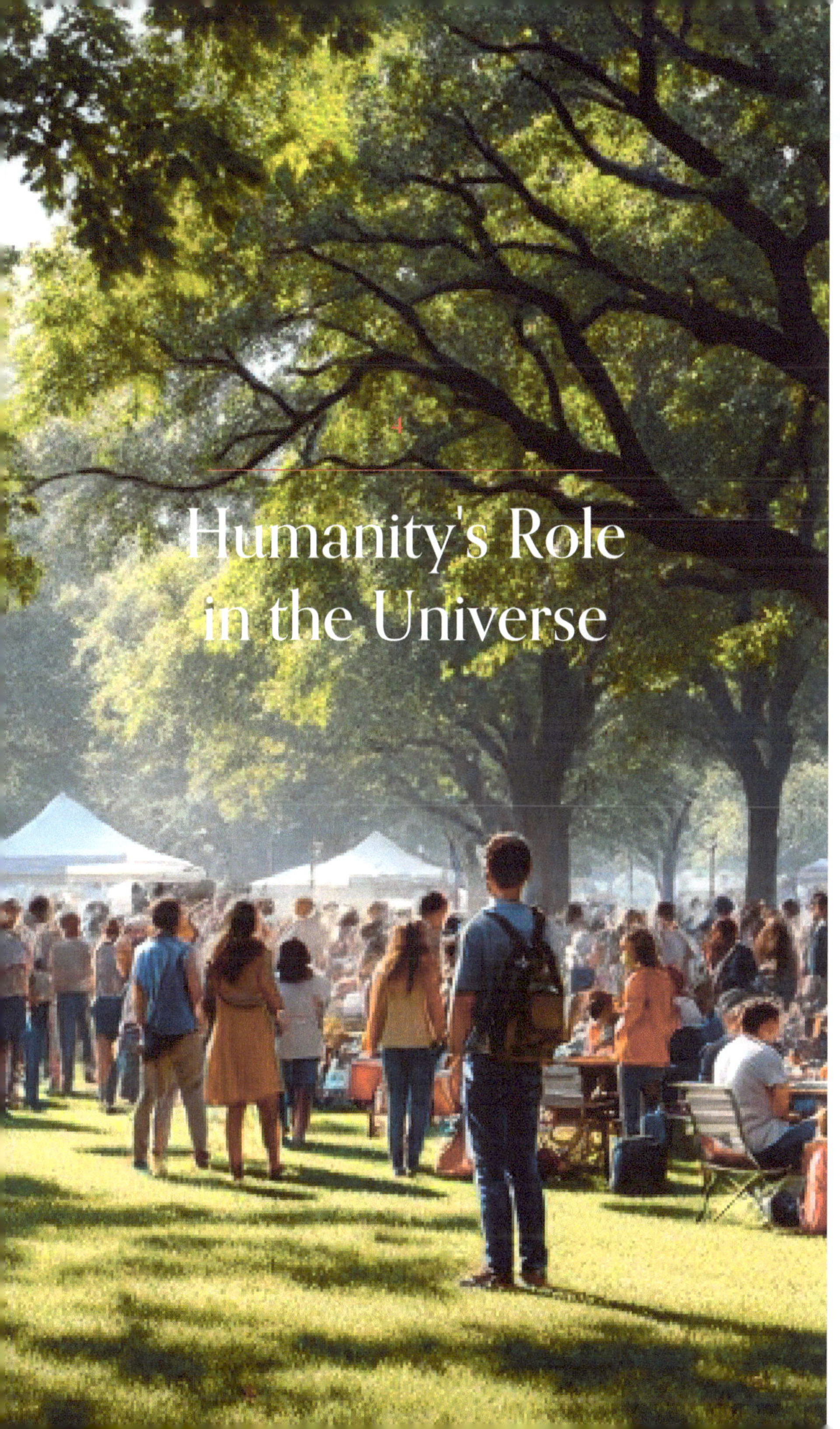
Humanity's Role
in the Universe

4.1 - Scientific Perspectives

In the boundless expanse of the universe, humanity gazes upward, seeking answers to age-old questions about our place within this vast cosmic tapestry. From ancient times, people have looked to the skies with a mixture of wonder and curiosity, pondering their connection to the stars. In India, these questions are woven into the fabric of our culture, where tales of celestial bodies and divine creation shape our understanding of existence. Each night, as children peer at the glittering sky, parents pass down stories that blend science and spirituality, fueling imaginations and igniting a quest for knowledge.

Yet, despite the advances in scientific exploration and space technology, the profound question remains: what is humanity's true role in the cosmos? Our scientific achievements tell part of the story, tracing our evolution from stardust to sentient beings capable of introspection and inquiry. However, science only sketches the outlines of our cosmic portrait. This chapter embarks on an exploration of humanity's place in the universe through diverse lenses—scientific, philosophical, and religious—revealing complex narratives that go beyond mere survival, inviting readers to consider not just where we came from, but why we exist and what responsibilities we hold in this awe-inspiring universe.

Humans, evolving from the very fabric of the universe, exist as tangible pieces of cosmic history. From the explosions of ancient stars came the elements that saturate our bodies—carbon, oxygen, nitrogen. Human beings are more than mere inhabitants of Earth; we are reminders of a grand cosmos tirelessly at work. This deep connection positions us within a framework where we are not only part of Earth's complex systems but are also wired to explore beyond its confines.

Scientific understanding highlights our tie to the universe through cosmic evolution. Life as we know it formed through a series of transformative cosmic events. Stars that lived and died billions of years ago created the elements which now constitute our bodies. This stardust composition places humans in a compelling narrative played out over eons. It's a story where the cosmos and biology fuse, demonstrating how intimately connected we are to this universal timeline.

Humans follow laws of physics; however, there's something remarkable about the human species. We veer beyond simple existence, thriving in awareness and understanding. Our universe, governed by unchanging physical principles, permits life forms capable of introspection and innovation. Beyond simply surviving, humans show curious tendencies to question, explore, and construct ideas about our universe. This intrinsic consciousness sets foundations for contemplation about existence.

Discoveries throughout history have enabled us to explore the cosmos and understand our place in the universe. Consider the stardust narrative itself—it is

galaxies light-years away, Hubble becomes a narrator singing the saga that began billions of years ago. Missions like Voyager and Mars rovers reflect humanity's resolve not merely to observe but diligently to seek out answers. These explorations serve to feed a growing curiosity that seems hardwired into the

part of a progressive unveiling of our cosmic origins. Through scientific advancements, humans launched space missions to go beyond our planet and peer closer at the universe. Space explorations decode secrets written in the cosmos—whether it's analyzing lunar rocks or studying extraterrestrial atmospheres.

Technological leaps such as the Hubble Space Telescope have broadened our cosmic view. By capturing images of

human experience.

Our consciousness and self-awareness, setting us apart in the animal kingdom, are crucial to understanding our unique roles. As observers and explorers, we embark on cosmic inquiries. Conscious of our place in the universe, humans do more than cling to survival. We relentlessly chase knowledge. Notable breakthroughs like landing on the moon stand testament to our capability to dream beyond Earth's borders. They illustrate an unyielding quest to understand who we are and why we exist.

Travel to Mars is becoming a reality. As missions gear up to explore the red planet, our identity as pioneers becomes evident. By sending rovers, humans venture on Mars without setting foot there, embodying our explorer spirit. These scientific feats demonstrate a deeper consciousness, urging exploration, both terrestrial and cosmic.

Hubert Reeves points to our ability to ponder our very existence. Consider Galileo, who dared to challenge deep-rooted geocentric beliefs. He brought forth a vision of the universe where Earth wasn't the sole center. His scientific courage models our ongoing journey—questioning, risking, and furthering our cosmic understanding. Reeves reminds us that our scientific and philosophical pursuits intertwine, nurturing a uniquely human narrative.

Yet, this embrace of scientific discovery sustains its distinct identity within the larger bounds of our roles. It's why scientists eagerly await telescopes focusing on potentially habitable exoplanets. It's why missions to asteroids and comets look back upon the early solar system, hoping for clues. Their endeavors place us in the universe philosophically—a humble part eager to celebrate the past while daring to imagine futures.

New technologies keep defining new aspects of our universe. They practically reconfigure narrations we thought we knew. Spectrometers on spacecraft analyze atmospheres looking for life markers; these tests bridge physics and the philosophical questions of "Is there anyone else?" Instruments, as they probe deeper, frequently bring us reflectively closer to grand inquiries on existence we habitually ponder. This intellectual bravery situates us as truth-seekers within cosmic panoramas.

Even as scientific roles unfold, there's an acknowledgment that answers don't end here. Humanity's existence encompasses ideologies grasping not only facts but meanings that stand beyond tangible measures. Science presents magnificent views on origins and capacities, nonetheless, questions remain about further contemplations not yet addressed through facts alone.

As this exploration concludes, the journey takes another direction. Scientific insights framed in cosmic evolution and personality merge with philosophical and religious considerations. They do more than codify theories—they inspire hope, proposing potential deeper narratives about humanity's role. While science brightly lights sections of our cosmic corridors, philosophical traditions extend conversations.

These traditions often define and question finer details of human existence and purpose. They ask what aims we should ascribe to this cosmic stage. Religious thought interacts by touching realms where ultimate meanings extend beyond empirical inquiries. These frameworks highlight humanity's potential responsibilities, grounded not only in understanding but respectful cohabitation within the universe.

In subsequent narratives, the spotlight shifts onto philosophical examinations and spiritual perspectives. They present views of humanity imbued with purposeful undertones striving to understand roles beyond systematic laws. Here, different aspects exchange dialogue on existence, extending beyond solemn rounds of the scientific journey. Thus, as this chapter transitions, we prepare to explore rooms where ethos and existential reflections echo, offering an enriched narrative of our cosmic belonging.

4.2 - Philosophical, Religious, and Human Experience Insights

Building on the scientific view of humanity as both a culmination and continuation of cosmic evolution, we find ourselves at a crossroads of discovery and meaning-making. From the vast galaxies down to the fundamental particles, the cosmos seems an endless dance of matter and energy. However, it is not only through scientific inquiry that we find our place. Philosophy and religion weave our quest for understanding with layers of purpose and responsibility.

Philosophically, humanity's role often shifts from mere observer to participant, part of a greater, layered hierarchy of existence. Philosophers have pondered whether our consciousness bestows upon us certain duties. Could it be that our ability to reason, create, and empathize makes us custodians of the universe's intrinsic values? Some philosophies suggest that just by virtue of existing, we are entangled in the ethical obligations to preserve, nurture, and cherish both life and the universe that houses us. For instance, utilitarian ethics focus on maximizing well-being, pushing humanity to act in ways that bring the greatest good for the greatest number. This perspective emphasizes our interconnectedness and the importance of considering the broader impact of our actions.

Religion brings another angle, viewing humans as central to divine plans or as spiritual beings with transcendent purposes. Different faiths attribute roles such as guardianship over Earth and its creatures as not only responsibilities but as means to honor a higher power. In Hindu philosophy, for example, the concept of 'dharma'—the guiding principle of cosmic order—encourages individuals to live according to their duties and responsibilities, which aligns with the belief that life should be lived in harmonious balance with the universe.

Religious viewpoints often propose humanity as the stewards of Earth, tasked with caring for the environment—a perspective echoed across traditions. Christianity, through the concept of stewardship, emphasizes that humans are caretakers of God's creation, accountable for maintaining the planet's well-being. In this narrative, ethical living, guided by principles such as love and compassion, becomes a sacred duty. Love, as presented in many religious traditions, serves a central role in fulfilling this responsibility. In Sikhism, the emphasis on love and justice underscores ethical behavior, promoting not mere passive existence but active participation in uplifting humanity and the world.

Across cultures, the intricate bond between love, compassion, and our responsibilities is a recurrent theme. In Buddhism, compassion forms the heart of ethical conduct, illustrating the belief that empathy toward others and the environment is essential for personal and collective enlightenment.

In examining humanity's ethical and spiritual responsibilities, we see diverse interpretations influenced by cultural contexts. Indigenous belief systems often highlight the deep interconnectedness between human beings and nature. For instance, many Native American spiritual traditions teach that nature is not to be exploited, but revered, and instruct followers to take only what they need while ensuring they leave enough for future generations.

The intrinsically human experiences of love, creativity, and empathy transcend philosophical and religious boundaries, becoming shared values that underscore our purpose in the universe. Whether one views these as gifts of a higher power or emergent properties of our evolution, their importance cannot be overstated. These attributes encourage us to contribute positively to the world, fostering unity and continuity amid diversity.

Examining how different belief systems interpret our ethical obligations offers insight into the varied ways humanity defines significance. In Judaism, 'tikkun olam' represents the idea of repairing the world through action, aligning spiritual aspirations with social responsibility. Such notions foster a sense of agency, encouraging individuals to make meaningful contributions to society.

The contrast between these perspectives illustrates a common narrative: humanity's consciousness comes with an inherent responsibility to nurture and sustain, whether seen through scientific, philosophical, or religious lenses. By viewing

Love shapes the heart, creativity fuels the imagination, and empathy forms the bridge to shared experiences, offering young parents a blueprint for raising considerate and fulfilled individuals.

TRANSFORM-ED

the universe as a complex, interwoven tapestry, the realization dawns that every thread—each human action—contributes to its ultimate pattern.

In modern times, as the world faces unprecedented ecological and social challenges, these ethical considerations become more urgent. Our conscious role as agents of change emphasizes that progress should not come at the expense of empathy and ethical responsibility. Whether inspired by sacred texts or philosophical contemplation, the drive to act with love and compassion remains a central theme.

Indian philosophical and spiritual traditions richly contribute to this dialogue. The teachings of the Bhagavad Gita, for example, present a vision of duty that transcends personal gain, urging one to act with awareness and integrity. This sense of responsibility speaks to the heart of shared human experience, encouraging action driven by inner values rather than external rewards.

Humanity's place in the cosmos often feels like a mosaic of perceptions and beliefs, each piece contributing to a deeper understanding. As we reflect on our roles as observers and caretakers of the universe, a tapestry of meaning unfurls—one woven from generations of philosophical inquiry, religious devotion, and cultural wisdom. Through this multifaceted lens, we recognize the unity of life, the sacredness of our relationships, and the shared journey in nurturing the universe.

Ultimately, the call is universal: to live with purpose, guided by the transcendent values of love, empathy, and responsibility. This call answers not only philosophical questions but addresses the urgency of our shared humanity. Whether we view ourselves as small parts of a vast cosmic machine or as spiritual beings with a higher purpose, our actions leave lasting imprints, resonating across the fabric of time and space.

Now that we understand humanity's profound connection to the cosmos through science, philosophy, and religion, we can embrace our roles as thoughtful caretakers of the universe. As Indian parents, you hold a special responsibility to impart this wisdom to future generations, nurturing curiosity, empathy, and respect for all life. By encouraging children to wonder about their place in the universe, you cultivate a mindset of stewardship and compassion. This ensures they grow into informed, responsible individuals who cherish the environment and contribute positively to society. With this knowledge, let us lead by example, inspiring actions rooted in love, wisdom, and responsibility. Together, fostering an awareness of our cosmic story will empower young minds, kindling a spirit of exploration and shared purpose essential for facing future challenges.

Notes

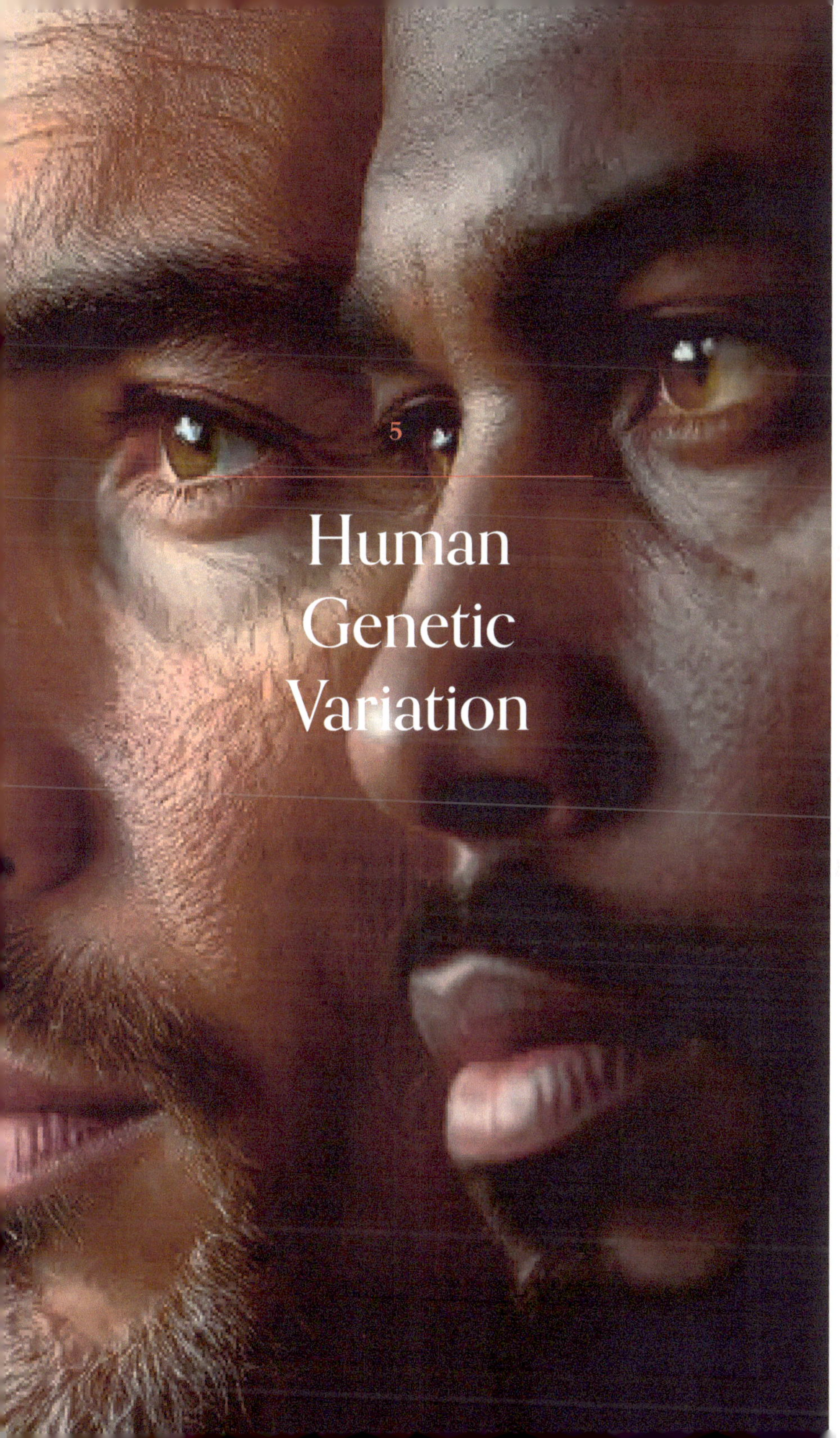

Human Genetic Variation

5.1 - Genomic Differences

Understanding the genomic differences between humans and within human populations is crucial for grasping our evolutionary history and biological diversity. Here's a breakdown:

Human Genetic Variation Within a Population:

High Similarity:

Humans are remarkably alike. On average, the genomes of any two people differ by approximately 0.1%. This means we share about 99.9% of our DNA.

Types of Differences:

These small variations include:

SNPs (Single Nucleotide Polymorphisms): Single base-pair changes.

Indels (Insertions/Deletions): Small insertions or deletions of DNA sequences.

CNVs (Copy Number Variations): Differences in the number of copies of certain DNA segments.

Impact:

These variations contribute to:

Physical differences (eye color, height, etc.).

Varied susceptibility to diseases.

Different responses to medications.

Genomic Differences Between Humans and Apes:

Chimpanzees: Our Closest Relatives:

Humans and chimpanzees share a common ancestor.

Estimates of genetic difference vary, but considering all forms of genomic variation, it's around 4%. This includes:

Base-pair substitutions.

Insertions and deletions.

Changes in gene regulation.

Other Apes:

Genetic divergence increases with gorillas, orangutans, and bonobos.

How These Differences Affect Us:

Although the percentage difference seems small, it results in significant distinctions:

Brain Development: Major differences in brain size and cognitive abilities. This is heavily influenced by differences in gene regulation.

Language: The capacity for complex language.

Bipedalism: Walking upright.

Social Behavior: Complex social structures.

Gene Regulation: It is important to know that changes in when and where genes are expressed plays a very large role in the differences between humans and apes.

5.2 - Key Considerations

Gene Regulation:

It's not just the DNA sequence itself, but how genes are regulated (when and

where they're turned on or off) that plays a critical role. Changes in gene regulation have had a very large impact on human evolution.

Evolutionary Significance:
Even small genetic changes can

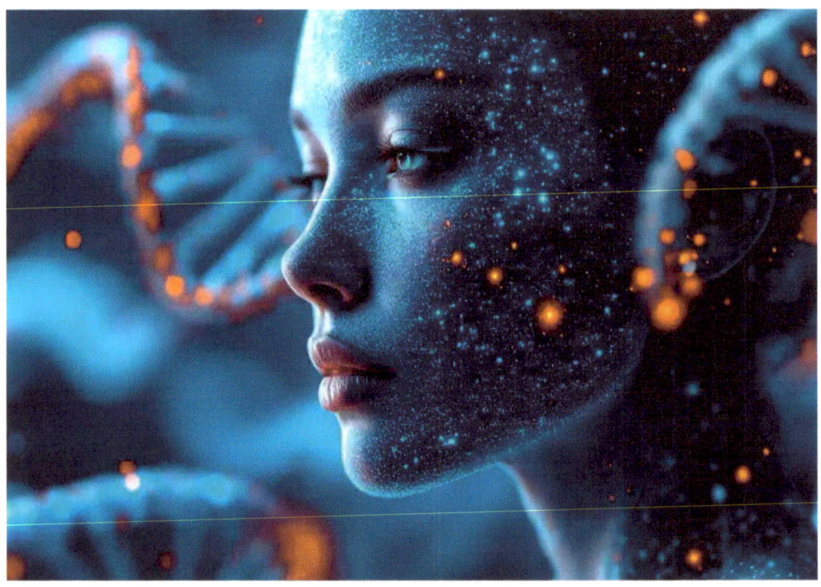

have significant effects on an organism's development and characteristics.

We share about 99.9% of our DNA

The 0.1% variations contribute to: Physical differences (eye color, height, etc.), Varied susceptibility to diseases, different responses to medications …

The
interconnectedness
of our DNA serves
as a foundation
for advocating an
upbringing rooted in
empathy and shared
human experience,
more conducive to
societal fulfillment
than competition.

The Power of Self-Compassion

6.1 - The Power of Self-Compassion

The power of self-compassion signifies a transformative capacity that many overlook in their daily strives for perfection. This chapter delves into the intricate dynamics between self-criticism and self-compassion, particularly in Indian society where achievement often overshadows personal well-being. By exploring the detrimental effects of relentless self-evaluation and external judgment, readers are drawn into an understanding of how habitual self-criticism can lead to a cycle of negativity. The chapter emphasizes that this constant self-scrutiny is not merely a personal flaw but a reflection of deeply ingrained societal norms and expectations, often starting from a young age. As individuals grow, these pressures manifest through continuous comparisons and societal benchmarks that stress accomplishment over genuine happiness or fulfillment.

We will discuss how adopting self-compassion as an alternative approach can fundamentally reshape one's perception of self-worth. Central to this exploration is the understanding that self-compassion is not about ignoring faults or embracing mediocrity; rather, it involves recognizing personal struggles with kindness and empathy. This perspective shift encourages people to treat themselves with the same understanding they would extend to a close friend experiencing difficulties. Throughout the chapter, strategies for cultivating this mindset are highlighted, including mindfulness practices and acknowledging shared humanity. By juxtaposing traditional societal measures of success with the benefits of self-compassion, readers are guided to appreciate the long-term advantages of nurturing a compassionate relationship with oneself. Ultimately, this chapter provides insights into fostering resilience and well-being by promoting a balanced and nurturing self-view amidst societal structures that often emphasize relentless ambition.

6.2 - The Impact of Societal Structures on Self-Worth

In today's Indian society, the influence of societal pressures on self-worth is profound. From a young age, individuals are often molded by their immediate environment, particularly through parental expectations and criticisms. Indian parents, in their quest to see their children succeed, sometimes set expectations that, while well-intentioned, may inadvertently lead to feelings of inadequacy. For example, when parents frequently compare their children to others or criticize them for not meeting certain academic or career milestones, it can create a foundation of self-doubt. These actions instill a belief in children that they must constantly strive for perfection to be worthy of love and acceptance.

As these children grow, they encounter broader social norms and cultural competitiveness that magnify these feelings. In India, where success is commonly measured by academic and financial achievements, unattainable standards are self-worth is measured against unrealistic ideals.

Furthermore, the continuous bombardment of societal judgments exacerbates this issue. In both urban and rural settings, judgments—whether from family, neighbors, or through the pervasive

often presented as the norm. The rigorous education system, coupled with the high value placed on prestigious careers like medicine or engineering, sets benchmarks that are difficult for many to achieve. As a result, individuals who do not meet these standards may feel they have failed, regardless of their talents or interests in other fields. This culture of competitiveness stresses accomplishment over personal growth, leading to an environment where reach of social media—perpetuate a cycle of harsh self-criticism. When individuals witness constant appraisals and critiques about appearance, career choices, or lifestyle through online platforms, it reinforces the notion that they are being perpetually evaluated. Consequently, many adopt self-criticism as a coping mechanism, believing it will drive them towards improvement. However, this approach often backfires by fostering a negative self-dialogue that neither supports mental health nor personal development.

As adults, this ingrained behavior impacts their perception of success. Society's definition of achievement is heavily skewed towards external validation rather than intrinsic fulfillment. Many adults find themselves trapped in careers or pursuits that externally appear successful but leave them feeling unfulfilled. The approval of peers, accolades, and tangible rewards become benchmarks of success, overshadowing the importance of personal satisfaction and happiness. This can lead to a disconnect between one's inner desires and outward accomplishments, contributing to long-term dissatisfaction and stress.

The cycle of seeking validation and equating self-worth with societal approval can be detrimental, leading to burnout and a lack of self-compassion. Understanding the influence of these societal pressures is crucial. By recognizing how deeply embedded these notions are, individuals can begin to challenge and redefine their metrics for self-worth. Moving beyond external measures, it becomes essential to cultivate a mindset that values personal growth, emotional well-being, and self-acceptance.

6.3 - Embracing Self-Compassion as an Alternative

In today's fast-paced world, it is easy to get caught up in a cycle of self-criticism. Many individuals, especially Indian parents and teenagers, are driven by the desire to succeed academically or professionally, often perpetuating a culture of fierce self-critique. It is crucial to understand that adopting self-compassion can significantly transform this negative self-perception into a more balanced and nurturing viewpoint. By advocating for self-compassion over self-criticism, we unlock the potential for a healthier mental and emotional state.

Self-compassion begins with acknowledging one's suffering and responding with kindness. When you face a difficult situation, such as receiving lower grades on an exam or falling short in some personal goal, your initial reaction might be one of disappointment. Instead of spiraling into negative self-talk, pause and recognize your feelings of hurt or frustration as valid. This mindful acknowledgment allows you to treat yourself with the same kindness as you would a close friend who is struggling. Whether it's allowing yourself to rest, indulging in activities you enjoy, or simply giving yourself time to heal, these small acts of kindness can make a substantial difference.

Practicing mindfulness is another vital step in fostering self-compassion.

Mindfulness encourages you to observe your thoughts and feelings without judgment. Imagine sitting quietly, focusing on your breathing, and gently noticing any critical self-comments as they arise. Instead of attaching to these thoughts and letting them define you, acknowledge them and let them pass like clouds in the sky. This practice creates a psychological space where self-acceptance can thrive. Over time, it becomes easier to embrace both your positive attributes and your areas for improvement without harsh judgment. By observing yourself objectively, you cultivate acceptance and pave the way for a balanced view of yourself.

Recognizing shared humanity further aids in overcoming self-criticism. Often, when facing difficulties, there's a tendency to feel isolated, as if you're the only one undergoing hardships. However, understanding that struggles are universal can be incredibly liberating. When realizing that everyone faces trials and tribulations, and that imperfections are part and parcel of being human, the burden of personal failings lightens considerably. This shared humanity fosters empathy not just toward others but also towards oneself, breaking down barriers of isolation and promoting a supportive community feeling.

A compassionate approach enables individuals to accept their strengths and weaknesses, facilitating personal growth. Through compassion, you learn to embrace imperfections as opportunities for learning rather than signs of failure. A student struggling with mathematics, for instance, may initially feel inadequate compared to peers. But through self-compassion, this student can shift perspective— acknowledging the challenge, seeking help, and recognizing progress, however small. By accepting weaknesses as natural and surmountable, and celebrating strengths even in modest achievements, a path of growth and self-improvement unfolds. Compassionate self-reflection thus plants seeds for a resilient, flourishing mentality.

To effectively incorporate self-compassion into daily life, it's essential to practice regularly. Begin by setting aside moments in your day dedicated to reflection. Write in a journal, noting instances where you felt critical of yourself, and consciously counter each criticism with a kind response. Consider joining mindfulness or meditation groups to build supportive networks that reinforce compassionate living. For those new to mindfulness, guided sessions using apps or online resources can be particularly helpful, providing structured support in cultivating awareness and acceptance. Remember, self-compassion isn't about indulging in self-pity or avoiding responsibility; rather, it involves approaching oneself with empathetic understanding and constructive intentions.

The transformation from self-criticism to self-compassion doesn't happen overnight. It requires patience, perseverance, and a willingness to engage deeply with oneself. Yet, the long-term benefits are profound. Individuals who practice self-compassion are often better equipped to handle stress, exhibit greater resilience in the face of challenges, and maintain healthier relationships with those around them. They become role models, demonstrating that true strength lies not in harsh self-assessment, but in compassionate self-awareness.

6.4 -Insights and Implications

iIn examining the pervasive societal pressures, it's evident that the ingrained culture of comparison and criticism deeply affects self-worth, especially among Indian families. This chapter has highlighted how unrealistic expectations foster a cycle of harsh self-assessment, rooted in generations of valuing external achievements over personal fulfillment. Many find themselves trapped, chasing validation through academic and career success, overshadowing their true desires and leading to long-term dissatisfaction. It's crucial for both parents and teenagers to challenge these norms, recognizing that worth is not solely defined by societal standards but also by personal growth and emotional well-being.

Introducing self-compassion as an alternative provides a transformative approach, shifting focus from relentless self-criticism to nurturing a kind and balanced self-view. By acknowledging shared humanity and practicing mindfulness, individuals can break the chains of negative self-dialogue and embrace their strengths and weaknesses alike. This shift not only fosters resilience but also enhances one's ability to handle stress and improve relationships. Cultivating this compassionate mindset requires dedication and practice, yet it promises profound benefits, offering a path to truly fulfilling lives based on inner strength and genuine self-appreciation.

The prevailing societal norms, emphasizing self-criticism over self-compassion, can inadvertently hinder a child's ability to develop a healthy self-esteem and a well-rounded personality.

Toolbox for Rhythm Building

Practical Tools & Resources

Visual Schedules

Family Meetings

Calming Techniques

Community Resources

Self-criticism to self-compassion

Embracing self-compassion for cultivating a strong mind

Self-criticism is self-defeating.

Self-criticism can be a starting point for self-compassion!

Speak to yourself in a more compassionate and supportive way.

Self-compassion is a practical way of treating yourself.

Accept ourselves for who we are!

Building Blocks of a Healthy Rhythm

Cultivating a Healthy Parenting Rhythm: Practical Strategies

Establish Predictable Routines

Consistent Responses

Regular Quality Time and Connection

Self-Care for Parents

Flexibility and Grace

High Fives

For strengthening mind

1	Personify your inner critic
2	Label the underlying emotions
3	Talk to yourself like a friend in need
4	Replace 'should' with 'could'
5	Think of mistakes as a science experiment

Have a strong mind

A mentally strong person shouldn't say:

1. "It's your fault."
2. "I don't care."
3. "That's your problem. Not mine."
4. "I'll do it myself."
5. "I don't care what anyone thinks."
6. "Because I said so."
7. "Failure's not an option."

The Rhythm of Parenting

7.1 - The Rhythm of Parenting

Jason watched as his daughter Ella, barely three, paced through the living room with determined steps, cradling her favorite stuffed toy. With every stumble she confidently righted herself, eyes wide with curiosity and resolve. Yet, there were moments where her small face clouded in frustration, when she encountered things beyond her reach or understanding. Jason realized that these early experiences were not just about learning to walk but navigating a much more complex journey—the emotional terrain of childhood. This wasn't just about taking care of her physical needs; it was about nurturing a balance between stepping in to guide and allowing her to explore the world in her own way.

This kind of parenting requires a keen sense of awareness and adaptability—traits that are becoming increasingly essential in an ever-evolving digital world where children like Ella grow up more tech-savvy than any previous generation. In this chapter, we delve into how intentional and adaptive parenting approaches can crucially impact a child's development, shaping their social skills and emotional intelligence, and ultimately preparing them for future challenges.

As we reach the conclusion of our exploration into modern parenting, it's essential to reflect on the themes that unify this journey. Parenting in today's world is more than a role—it's a dynamic dance that requires awareness, intentionality, and adaptability. Our children, who belong to Generation Z and Generation Alpha, are growing up in an era vastly different from any before, marked by rapid technological advancements, societal shifts, and global challenges. Through all these changes, one constant remains: the impact of intentional yet nuanced parenting on their emotional development and overall personality.

7.2 - Importance of Intentional Parenting

Parenting today isn't a one-size-fits-all journey. Each child is unique, and parents need to tailor their approaches to fit the emotional and developmental needs of their children. This tailored parenting holds significant sway in shaping a child into a well-rounded individual, especially when the approach is both intentional and subtle. While it might seem at first like finding the balance between guidance and independence is akin to walking a tightrope, taking a dynamic approach proves instrumental in nurturing emotional intelligence and social skills.

Consider the story of Lucy, a mother of a ten-year-old son, Alex. She discovered early on that Alex had an affinity for music but was also rather shy in social settings. By actively engaging with Alex about his interests and gently encouraging him to express himself, Lucy managed to create opportunities for Alex to step outside his comfort zone. For instance, she enrolled him in a local band class, which aligned well with his passion. Lucy's patient, emotionally intelligent approach encouraged Alex to blossom socially by meeting peers who shared his interests,

significantly from previous generations; they are digital natives, accustomed to technology that older generations never experienced at such a formative age. Parents need to delve into this generational insight to enhance parenting effectiveness. It's not about restricting technology but rather about striking a balance and integrating digital literacy into developing other life skills.

all without feeling overwhelmed. This is a classic example of how intentional parenting helps children enter social spheres with confidence, leveraging what they know and love.

In an age where parents often become competitors against gadgets for their children's attention, understanding the generational differences holds real value. Generation Z and Generation Alpha differ

Intentional parenting, particularly focusing on emotional growth, prepares children for future societal roles. When children learn appropriate ways to express emotions and understand others' perspectives, they are better equipped to navigate relationships and professional environments later on. Emotional intelligence directly impacts social capability. Here, the subtlety lies in parents allowing children to experience and express emotions rather than suppressing them. Realistically, the goal isn't to remove all adversity for children but to guide them on how to process challenges constructively.

Take Robert and Emily, who chose to incorporate empathy as a core value in their family. They regularly engaged in discussions with their children about the significance of kindness and empathy. By guiding their kids through real-world scenarios where both positive and negative emotions come into play, Robert and Emily's children learned how to empathize and connect with others. Their kids grew up to actively participate in community service and became well-rounded, engaged young adults. This life skill, nurtured through consistent yet flexible parenting, became a key component of their societal involvement.

Another critical dimension of intentional parenting is teaching children how to adapt their behavior in various social situations. Amid diverse social layers, parents play a vital role as facilitators. Don't underestimate the value of modeling positive interactions. When parents demonstrate patience, active listening, or problem solving in their day-to-day dealings, children absorb more than meets the eye. These lessons, though sometimes indirect, lay the groundwork for how children will approach situations independently in the future.

Intentional parenting also encompasses instilling values that are consistent and influential. Let's look at Samira, an advocate for environmental sustainability, who consistently shares this passion with her daughter, Maya. Samira involves Maya in activities, discussion, and projects that illuminate the importance of sustaining our planet. Through this unyielding value system taught with finesse, Maya brings an environmentally conscious approach to her school projects and everyday life. This kind of nuanced parenting underscores the sustainability of character development when guided by strong, demonstrated values.

Moreover, it's vital to realize the importance of not just being present but being effectively present. Allocating dedicated time to engage in open dialogue with children about their experiences, thoughts, and plans allows them to develop a sense of security and validation. In turn, this helps them view the world as a safe place for interaction and exploration, a notion that stands them in good stead throughout adulthood. By being receptive to their children's needs and adapting their parenting accordingly, parents could furnish a more enriching foundation for the children's endeavors.

Ultimately, parents need to embrace a parenting style that values flexibility while remaining rooted in core principles. By doing so, parents set a secure backdrop in which children can flourish. Consistent practices facilitate a textured understanding of the world for children, making them capable of transforming theoretical knowledge into practical application.

As this section transitions into exploring how flexible but consistent parenting accelerates development within a nurturing environment, the journey into child development continues. However, as you absorb these insights, remember that each child will grow into their unique rhythm. Effective parenting involves tuning into this rhythm and guiding children along as they evolve into confident, responsible, and active members of society. The subtle nuances of intentional parenting might take time to fully appreciate, but the long-term benefits speak for themselves.

7.3 -Flexible but Consistent Parenting

Intentional, value-driven parenting takes center stage as previous discussions highlighted its significance. It's becoming clear that while values guide us, the harmony of flexibility and consistency in parenting ensures those values take root. Let's consider how this combination fosters a nurturing environment where Gen Z and Gen Alpha thrive, creating not only a safe space but one of profound love and connection.

Parenting, especially today, demands adaptability. Yet, it's crucial for adaptability to stem from a solid base of values. Children, regardless of their generational label, respond positively to environments where warmth and security are consistent. Take the morning routine, for instance. A household where parents prioritize positive starts to the day sets a tone. Perhaps the family gathers for breakfast, sharing not just a meal but meaningful conversation, affirming each member's role and importance. This simple act can reflect deeper family values such as respect and togetherness. Consistency in this practice builds trust and sets a predictable rhythm kids rely on.

The psychological benefits for children in such environments cannot be understated. A child who knows they will be listened to, whose voice holds weight, grows with confidence. The consistency of knowing certain routines or rituals will always be there provides comfort and security. Children better process their emotions when they feel that their environment holds stability—even as it adapts to life's natural shifts. Emotional resilience begins to take root in these conditions.

In contrast, consider households where rules shift inexplicably or where expectations feel amorphous. Without a clear baseline of consistent values guiding behavior and attitudes, children struggle to find their footing. Their emotional development stalls as they expend energy trying to discern what's expected rather than embracing growth opportunities. On the flip side, rigid structures devoid of flexibility can stifle creativity and self-expression, leading children to feel trapped or misunderstood.

This is where the blend of being steadfast yet flexible becomes paramount. Imagine a family that prioritizes personal achievement but adjusts expectations to their child's unique talents and interests. Maybe one child excels athletically, while another sees their potential in arts. The consistent value of nurturing individual potential adapts in its execution, affirming for both children the stability of the family's support while recognizing their unique paths.

Furthermore, a structured evening, like shared dinners, can reinforce these family values. During this time, everyone can discuss their highs and lows, fostering connection through shared experience and collective reflection. It's a great opportunity to reiterate family values by praising acts of kindness or showing empathy, thereby modeling behavior in a practical setting. Over time, these discussions instill a sense of safety and belonging, empowering children to approach their world with confidence because they have a steady foundation from which to start each day.

Consistency in parenting also extends beyond the home into school settings. Establishing communication with educators ensures that the values nurtured at home are reinforced in the classroom. A family who values curiosity and learning should regularly engage with teachers to understand how their child is growing academically and socially. This partnership between parents and teachers offers a safety net for children, who see the collaborative effort to see them thrive.

As we navigate these discussions, it's important to remember that while routines and consistency build a nurturing environment, they also create room for joy and spontaneity. Finding predictability in day-to-day practices allows space for flexibility when unexpected moments of joy arise. Choosing a spontaneous family outing promotes joy and family bonding, reinforcing the value of balance in family life.

This rhythm of parenting will reduce anxiety and provide children greater emotional stability. Parents must model the essential balance between predictability and creativity, thus encouraging their children to do the same within safe, loving boundaries. Providing a springboard for them to explore their emotions or tackle new challenges, knowing they can rely on a supportive and resilient safety net at home.

Looking ahead, this stable foundation will play a crucial role in developing empathy and resilience. By creating an environment where love, safety, and structured flexibility thrive, children can engage meaningfully in their surroundings. The continuity and reassurance they feel at home will help them navigate complex social landscapes with emotional intelligence. They will become

Parenting is about finding harmony in the chaos and discovering the beat behind fostering emotional connections.

adept at understanding and responding to others' emotions, fueled by the empathy they've experienced and learned. Their resilience will grow as they have seen adaptability modeled positively, equipping them for a world that constantly shifts and evolves.

Thus, maintaining a rhythm in parenting not only nurtures immediate family bonds but also develops the emotional skills necessary to help children grow into kind, adaptive adults. When parents use their intentionality to guide stability and embrace change, they create a dynamic home environment capable of fostering enduring psychological and relational skills. In doing so, they not only prepare their children for what comes next, but they also enlighten us all on what it means to live harmoniously and joyfully within our communities.

7.4 -Role of Empathy and Resilience

Flexible but consistent parenting stands out as a keystone for developing a nurturing environment for children. This approach balances discipline with understanding, allowing children to explore their individuality while feeling secure in their boundaries. Children raised with such parenting styles often benefit from an environment that encourages their natural curiosity while maintaining a firm yet loving structure. This dual need for flexibility and consistency is particularly pivotal for nurturing empathy and resilience – essential traits in today's dynamic world.

Empathy, the ability to understand and share the feelings of others, can be cultivated from an early age. In the home, parents demonstrate empathy by actively listening to their children, validating their emotions, and showing compassion for their experiences. For example, when a child struggles with a friend at school, an empathetic parent discusses these feelings openly, helping the child navigate these complex emotions. Schools can reinforce these lessons by creating spaces where children collaborate, discuss, and engage in activities that put them in others' shoes. Projects that emphasize teamwork and community service can serve as practical applications, teaching children to consider perspectives beyond their own. This nurturing of empathy not only fosters harmonious relationships but also promotes emotional intelligence, allowing kids to handle life's ups and downs with grace.

Closely linked to empathy is resilience – the ability to recover from setbacks. Teaching resilience involves setting appropriate challenges for children, where failure is perceived as a learning opportunity rather than a dead end. Parents encourage resilience by setting realistic expectations and refraining from solving every problem for their children. For instance, when a child encounters difficulty with homework, a parent might offer guidance without providing direct answers, empowering the child to find solutions independently. In educational settings, resilience can be reinforced by incorporating lessons on growth mindset, where the focus shifts from innate talent to perseverance and effort. Such environments prepare children to face challenges with a confident and persistent attitude.

Creativity and critical thinking also have a symbiotic relationship with empathy and resilience. Creativity allows children to express themselves and their emotions in innovative ways, providing outlets that contribute to their mental well-being. Encouraging imaginative play, introducing children to different art forms, or simply allowing unstructured time for exploration can greatly enhance creativity. This unbridled expression enables children to channel emotions productively, leading to healthier coping mechanisms. Conversely, critical thinking teaches children to analyze and question their world, encouraging them to explore multiple viewpoints and problem-solve effectively.

At home, critical thinking can be nurtured through everyday activities like family discussions about books, news, or even planning trips. Parents can stimulate thoughtful conversation by asking open-ended questions that prompt their children to express opinions and reason, thereby honing their analytical skills. Schools can further this development by incorporating project-based learning, which challenges students to investigate real-world problems, encouraging them

to hypothesize, test, and draw conclusions. Such skills are invaluable, as they prepare children for an ever-evolving future where adaptability is key.

Logical thinking complements critical thinking by structuring a child's problem-solving approach. Parents can stimulate this by involving children in activities like building sets, puzzles, or strategy games, which require sequential thinking and planning. Teachers can extend this foundation in the classroom through engaging activities that incorporate logic puzzles or coding exercises. These experiences shape children into thinkers who can systematically approach problems, weighing evidence, and drawing reasoned conclusions.

As these skills flourish—empathy, resilience, creativity, and logical and critical thinking—their impact on a child's emotional development becomes evident. High self-awareness emerges as children learn to understand and manage their own emotions, leading to reduced anxiety. When children recognize and articulate their stressors and contributors to their happiness, they develop the tools to mitigate feelings of anxiety and cultivate inner peace.

High self-awareness and low anxiety pave the way for sustained joy—a key objective of effective parenting. Joy is not merely momentary happiness, but a profound sense of well-being and contentment that persists. Parents can encourage sustained joy by celebrating effort as much as achievement, nurturing a love for learning. Sharing in their child's interests and enthusiasm can ignite passion, while simple activities like family game nights or nature walks foster belonging and happiness. Schools that emphasize character education, focusing on the joy of discovery and collaboration, further extend this environment.

The ultimate manifestation of flexible but consistent parenting is a nurturing environment that seamlessly integrates home and school experiences. In practice, this might mean parents and educators maintaining open lines of communication, ensuring values taught at home are reflected and reinforced in school. When a child sees collaboration between parents and educators working towards their well-being, it strengthens the trust they place in both and the lessons they impart.

Ultimately, the journey of parenting reimagines evolving landscapes and perspectives. Empathy and resilience, when nurtured with creativity and critical thinking, foster children who are well-rounded intellectually and emotionally. Flexible yet consistent parenting is more than just a philosophy; it's a roadmap guiding children towards a future brimming with potential, resilience, and joy. By thoughtfully applying these principles, parents and educators alike contribute to raising a generation equipped to flourish, no matter the challenges they face.

Concluding Thoughts

As we grasp the profound impact of parenting methods on child development

and well-being, it becomes evident that our journey as parents requires a blend of intentionality, flexibility, and empathy. By embracing these principles, we not only foster emotional intelligence and resilience in our children but also prepare them to navigate social landscapes with confidence. Understanding the uniqueness of each child allows us to tailor our approaches, ensuring they thrive in environments that balance guidance with independence. Now that we recognize the importance of consistent routines paired with adaptable strategies, we can create nurturing spaces where Gen Z and Gen Alpha flourish, equipped for the challenges of a dynamic world. Embracing this approach means fostering the growth of well-rounded, empathetic individuals ready to contribute positively to society.

As we reach the conclusion of our exploration into modern parenting, it's essential to reflect on the themes that unify this journey. Parenting in today's world is more than a role—it's a dynamic dance that requires awareness, intentionality, and adaptability. Our children, who belong to Generation Z and Generation Alpha, are growing up in an era vastly different from any before, marked by rapid technological advancements, societal shifts, and global challenges. Through all these changes, one constant remains: the impact of intentional yet nuanced parenting on their emotional development and overall personality.

At the heart of effective parenting lies the principle of creating rhythm and harmony within the family structure. This approach isn't about rigidity; it's about finding balance and being attuned to our children's evolving needs. By fostering a nurturing environment based on demonstrated values, we can support our children's growth while ensuring they have the safety and security necessary for healthy emotional and social development. This equilibrium allows them to thrive as responsible, empathetic, and resilient individuals.

In our quest to nurture empathy and resilience—two of the most crucial traits—we plant seeds that will flourish throughout their lives. Empathy enables children to relate to others, understand diverse perspectives, and foster genuine connections. Resilience equips them with the strength to navigate challenges, adapt to change, and bounce back from setbacks. Together, these qualities form the foundation of a well-rounded individual capable of contributing positively to society.

The role of love, affection, and attachment cannot be overstated. When children feel secure in their familial bonds, they develop deep-rooted confidence in themselves and their abilities. Maintaining and reestablishing these connections when deviations occur ensures that our children grow up in a stable environment where they are valued and understood. Such an approach not only enriches family ties but also extends to schools and communities, creating circles of support that envelop our children in warmth and guidance.

As young parents, you hold the key to teaching your children how to learn—a skill far more enduring than any single piece of knowledge. Encouraging high self-awareness and a consciousness that embraces creativity, critical thinking, and logical reasoning prepares them to thrive in an ever-evolving world. It is through learning to learn that children unlock their potential, able to think independently, question norms, and innovate solutions.

To achieve this vision, home and school must work in tandem, acting as pillars of support and engines of growth. By actively engaging in your children's educational journeys, you help pave pathways where curiosity is celebrated, and mistakes are viewed as opportunities for growth. Schools should complement this environment, nurturing talents and encouraging exploration, fostering spaces where children can express their ideas freely.

Ultimately, the rhythm of parenting must lead to reduced anxiety and sustained joy. In fostering such an environment, we set the stage for children to blossom into joyful, well-adjusted adults capable of contributing meaningfully to the world around them. The goal of parenting should not be perfection but presence—being present for milestones, setbacks, discoveries, and daily joys. It is in these moments that true connection and understanding are forged.

This journey of parenting is as transformative for us as it is for our children. As we guide them towards becoming fine human beings, we too evolve, gaining new insights and developing deeper empathy. It's a shared

voyage filled with lessons, love, laughter, and occasional challenges, all of which shape us into better versions of ourselves. Through reflective and compassionate parenting, you are sculptors of the future.

You are nurturing the minds and hearts that will lead generations to come. Embrace the tools and insights offered in this book to cultivate relationships that flourish on trust, respect, and understanding.

In closing, let us remember that parenting is not a static endeavor. It's a rhythmic dance, ever-changing, requiring courage, patience, and grace. Approach each day with a willingness to listen and learn, to love unconditionally, and to adapt as needed. The legacy we leave behind will not be built on monumental actions but on the accumulation of everyday efforts that reinforce the enduring power of empathetic, resilient, and intentional parenting.

As you embark on this incredible journey, embrace the unpredictability, cherish the joyous moments, and find solace in knowing that your dedication shapes a future of hope and promise. Let the rhythm of parenting guide you, confident in your ability to nurture the next generation of compassionate, innovative, and thoughtful leaders.

The benefits of healthy parenting rhythm

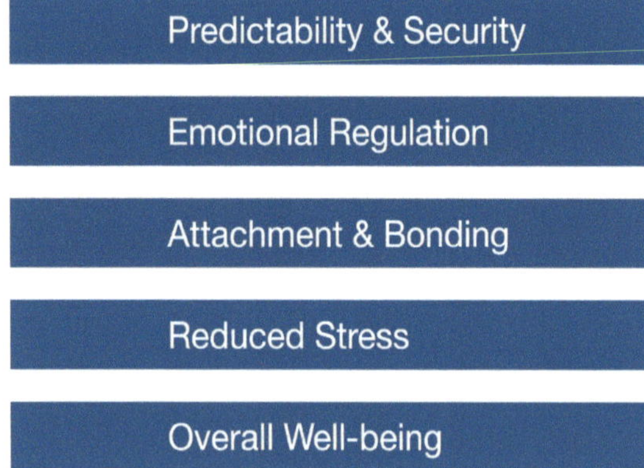

Our efforts to cultivate a healthier parenting rhythm

Where do we stand?

Scan to attempt quiz

Notes

Attribute
Attribute
Attainment
Attainment
Accolades
Accolades
Attention
Attention
Acceptance
Acceptance
Affection
Affection

Notes

Notes

Rhythm of Parenting

Parenting is not a static endeavour. It's a rhythmic dance, ever-changing, requiring courage, patience, and grace. Approach each day with a willingness to listen and learn, to love unconditionally, and to adapt as needed.

Transform-Ed